UPDOG

IN THE SPOTLIGHT

BILLIE EILISH

CHART-TOPPING ARTIST

Heather E. Schwartz

Lerner Publications ◆ Minneapolis

Lerner Publications Company
An imprint of Lerner Publishing Group, Inc.
241 First Avenue North
Minneapolis, MN 55401 USA

For reading levels and more information, look up this title at www.lernerbooks.com.

Main body text set in ITC Franklin Gothic Std.
Typeface provided by Adobe Systems.

Designer: Viet Chu

Library of Congress Cataloging-in-Publication Data

Names: Schwartz, Heather E., author.
Title: Billie Eilish: chart-topping artist / Heather E. Schwartz.
Description: Minneapolis : Lerner Publications, 2023. | Series: In the spotlight (Updog books) | Includes bibliographical references and index. | Audience: Ages 8–11 | Audience: Grades 4–6 | Summary: "Billie Eilish dominated the 2020 Grammys, winning five awards. But she was just getting started. Learn about Eilish's love of music, her personal life, and much more!"—Provided by publisher.
Identifiers: LCCN 2021054006 (print) | LCCN 2021054007 (ebook) | ISBN 9781728458380 (library binding) | ISBN 9781728463698 (paperback) | ISBN 9781728461755 (ebook)
Subjects: LCSH: Eilish, Billie, 2001– —Juvenile literature. | Singers—United States—Biography—Juvenile literature.
Classification: LCC ML3930.E35 S28 2022 (print) | LCC ML3930.E35 (ebook) | DDC 782.42164092 [B]—dc23

LC record available at https://lccn.loc.gov/2021054006
LC ebook record available at https://lccn.loc.gov/2021054007

Manufactured in the United States of America
1-50867-50204-3/14/2022

TABLE OF CONTENTS

Billie's Beginning

Billie Eilish's eyes went wide, and she covered her face.

She'd won the 2021 Record
of the Year Grammy Award.

Billie wrote her first song at the age of eleven.
She also wrote songs with her brother, Finneas.

They worked on "Ocean Eyes" together. The song went viral.

UP NEXT!
Rising star.

Creating a Career

When she was fourteen years old,
Billie landed a record deal.

She released her first EP in 2017.

EP: a recording that contains several songs but fewer than an album

Billie went on tour.

UP NEXT!

Under pressure.

In the Spotlight

Billie was open about her life.
She talked about her feelings.

STAR STATS

Full name: Billie Eilish Pirate Baird O'Connell

Date of birth: December 18, 2001

Hometown: Los Angeles, California

HONORS:

Hit No. 1 on the *Billboard* Hot 100 chart with her song "Bad Guy"

Won five Grammy Awards in 2020

Was *Billboard's* 2020 Top Female Artist

She said she had
Tourette's syndrome.

Tourette's syndrome:
a medical condition
that causes sudden tics,
movements, or sounds

She said she wore baggy clothes so people would focus on her art and not her looks.

UP NEXT!

Growing stronger.

Moving Forward

Billie's first album was a huge hit.

After it came out, she talked about her anxiety and depression.

anxiety: a medical condition that causes someone to feel fear or nervousness about what might happen

depression: a medical condition that causes someone to feel sad and hopeless

In 2021, Billie was ready for a change. She tried wearing different kinds of clothing.

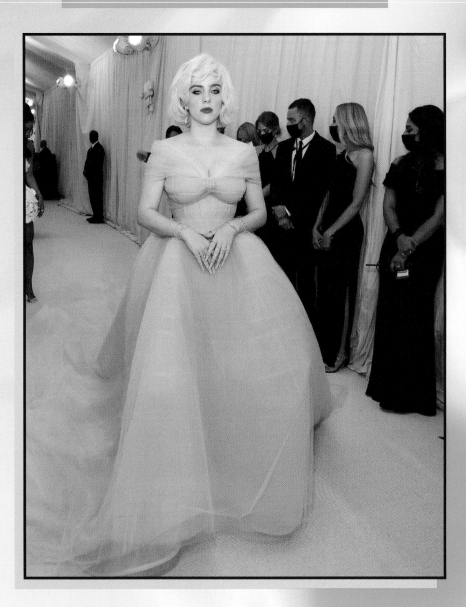

She opened up on her album
Happier Than Ever. She sang
about dealing with fame.

Billie loves sharing her
music and life with her fans.

Just like Billie

Billie opens up to people to help herself and others. How could talking openly help others and yourself?

GLOSSARY

anxiety: a medical condition that causes someone to feel fear or nervousness about what might happen

depression: a medical condition that causes someone to feel sad and hopeless

EP: a recording that contains several songs but fewer than an album

Tourette's syndrome: a medical condition that causes sudden tics, movements, or sounds

CHECK IT OUT!

Biography: Billie Eilish
https://www.biography.com/musician/billie-eilish

Britannica Kids: Anxiety
https://kids.britannica.com/students/article/anxiety
/316422

Honders, Christine. *Depression*. New York: Rosen, 2021.

KidsHealth: Tourette Syndrome
https://kidshealth.org/en/kids/k-tourette.html

London, Martha. *Billie Eilish*. Lake Elmo, MN: Focus
Readers, 2020.

Schwartz, Heather E. *Olivia Rodrigo: Hit Singer-Songwriter*.
Minneapolis: Lerner Publications, 2023.

INDEX

PHOTO ACKNOWLEDGMENTS

Image credits: Kevin Winter/Getty Images, pp. 4–5; Kevin Mazur/ Getty Images, pp. 6, 15; Angela Weiss/AFP/Getty Images, p. 7; Araya Doheny/WireImage/Getty Images, p. 8; Craig Barritt/ Stringer/Getty Images, p. 9; C Flanigan/WireImage/Getty Images, p. 10; AP Photo/Jack Plunkett/Invision, p. 11; Amy Harris/Shutterstock.com, p. 12; Scott Dudelson/Stringer/Getty Images, p. 14; Steve Russell/Toronto Star/Getty Images, p. 16; Mike Coppola/Getty Images, p. 17; Arturo Holmes/MG21/Getty Images, p. 18; Gary Miller/WireImage/Getty Images, p. 19; Rich Fury/Getty Images, p. 20. Design elements: Medesulda/Getty Images; oxygen/Getty Images.

Cover: Amy Harris/Shutterstock.com.